http://www.lyrics.co.nz/

W9-APE-830

KENYA
AFRICA'S TAMED WILDERNESS

DISCOVERING our HERITAGE

By Joann J. Burch

DILLON PRESS
New York

Maxwell Macmillan Canada
Toronto

Maxwell Macmillan International
New York Oxford Singapore Sydney

Acknowledgments

With thanks to Professor Hartmut S. Walter, Department of Geography, the University of California, Los Angeles, for his assistance.

Photo Credits
Cover image courtesy of Y. Lehmann/United Nations Photo
Interior: Robert Perkins, 8-9, 40, 60, 70; United Nations Photo, 13, 55, 64-65; Joann Burch, 16, 37, 81; Karen Beardsley, 20, 33, 42, 85, 87, 95, 103; Dr. Jamie Monson, 23, 75, 91, 98-99; Beverly Houwing, 28-29; Herbert Kraus, 45; Library of Congress, 49; Shawn Alston, 67, 76; Judith Helfand, 109; Dr. Ed Karanja, 116; Kenya coat of arms by Veronica Cherniak.

The following publishers have generously given permission to reprint tales from copyrighted works: "Never Ask Me about My Family" from *African Folktales,* by Roger D. Abrahams. Copyright 1983 by Roger D. Abrahams. Reprinted by permission of Pantheon Books, a division of Random House, Inc. "A Man Who Could Transform Himself" from *Akamba Stories,* by John S. Mbiti. Copyright 1966 by Oxford University Press. Reprinted by permission of Oxford University Press.

Library of Congress Cataloging-in-Publication Data
Burch, Joann Johansen.
　　Kenya : Africa's tamed wilderness / Joann J. Burch.
　　　　　p.　cm. — (Discovering our heritage)
　　Includes bibliographical references.
　　Summary: Describes the geography, people, history, folklore, family life, food, schools, and sports of Kenya, as well as its immigrants to the United States.
　　ISBN 0–87518–512–6
　　1. Kenya—Juvenile literature. [1. Kenya.] I. Title. II. Series.
DT433.522.B87 1992　　　　　　　　　　　　　　　　　　91–43104
967.62 – dc20

Dillon Press　　　　　　　　　　　　　Maxwell Macmillan Canada, Inc.
Macmillan Publishing Company　　　　1200 Eglinton Avenue East
866 Third Avenue　　　　　　　　　　Suite 200
New York, NY　10022　　　　　　　　Don Mills, Ontario M3C 3N1

Macmillan Publishing Company is part of the Maxwell Communication Group of Companies.

First edition

Printed in the United States of America

10　9　8　7　6　5　4　3　2　1

Contents

Fast Facts about Kenya

Official Name: Jamhuri ya Kenya, Republic of Kenya
Capital: Nairobi
Location: On the Indian Ocean coast of East Africa, straddling the equator. Countries that border Kenya are Ethiopia and the Sudan on the north, Somalia on the east, Tanzania on the south, and Uganda on the west.
Area: 224,960 square miles (582,646 square kilometers). Kenya has 300 miles (483 kilometers) of coastline.
Elevation: *Highest:* Mount Kenya—17,058 feet (5,174 meters); *Lowest:* Sea level
Population: 25,393,000 (1990 estimate). *Distribution:* 20 percent urban (1986 estimate), 80 percent rural (1986 estimate)
Births (per 1,000 population, 1989): 51. Deaths (per 1,000 population, 1989): 9. Population increase per year: 4.2 percent, the highest in the world.
Form of Government: A republic headed by a president. He selects the vice president and 20 cabinet ministers from the 170 members of the one-house National Assembly. All but 12 of the members are elected to five-year terms. The president appoints the 12 members. He also appoints Kenya's judges.
Important Products: *Agriculture*—tea, coffee, maize,

wheat, cotton, sisal, sugar cane, pyrethrum; *Manufacturing* — cement, chemicals, light machinery, textiles, petroleum products; *Industries* — food and beverage processing, vehicle assembly and repair .

Basic Unit of Money: Kenyan shilling

Languages: Official languages — English and Swahili. Local languages are spoken by various ethnic groups.

Religion: 64 percent Christian, 30 percent traditional African religions, 6 percent Muslim

Flag: Three horizontal stripes, in black, red, and green, with a war shield on crossed spears in the center

National Anthem: "Wimbo wa Taifa" ("Anthem of the Nation")

National Motto: *Harambee* ("Let's pull together")

Major Holidays: New Year's Day; Good Friday and Easter Monday; Labor Day — May 1; *Madaraka* Day — June 1; *Eid al-Fitr* — at the end of Ramadan; Moi Day — October 10; Kenyatta Day — October 20; *Jamhuri* Day — December 12; Christmas Day; Boxing Day — December 26

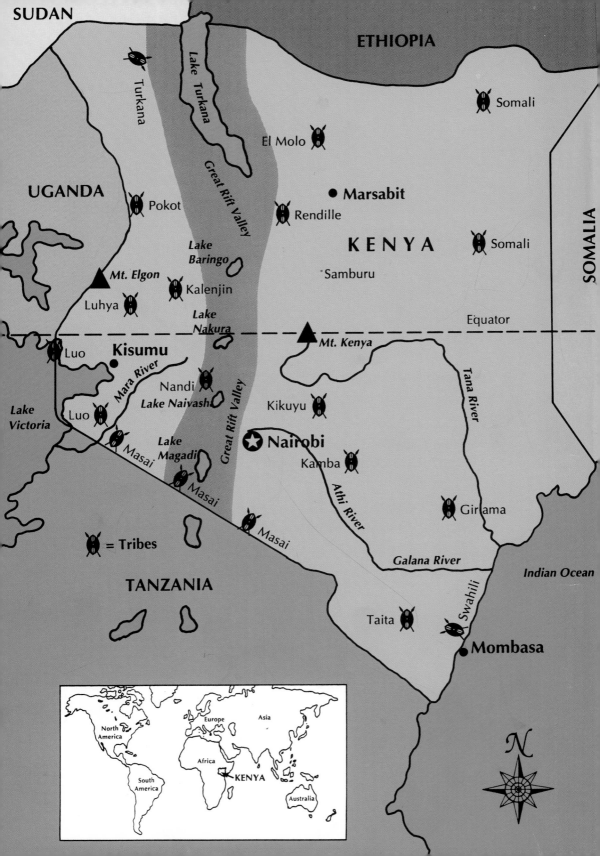

1. Animals Everywhere

Ahmed, the best-known elephant in Kenya, stands guard in the courtyard of the Nairobi Museum. He used to live on Mount Marsabit, an oasis in the middle of Kenya's northern desert. He was the most popular of the big-tusked elephants that browsed in the mist forests on the mountaintop. Ahmed was quite friendly, and he sometimes wandered into the town of Marsabit to sample the vegetables in people's gardens.

Ahmed became famous with the townspeople as well as with the nomads who came through town. Soon people throughout Kenya knew about the elephant's mischief. President Kenyatta appointed an honor guard of rangers to protect Ahmed for life. When the elephant died in 1974, his body was stuffed and sent to the Nairobi Museum. Since then, Ahmed has become the symbol for wildlife conservation in Kenya.

Kenya is one of the last places on earth where so many wild animals roam free. Herds of zebras and wildebeests travel across the savannah, the name for a broad area of grasslands. Lions lurk in the tall grass, waiting to pounce on any animal that has straggled away from the herd. Groups of elephants spray them-

Zebra roam the savannah near the Tanzania border.

selves with water at water holes or beside streams. Hippopotamuses snooze in swamps or in water along the banks of rivers and lakes. Almost anywhere you go in Kenya there are animals — either wildlife or the livestock of nomads and herdsmen.

Kenya's wild animals have become a national treasure. Tourists come from all over the world to see the wildlife. Besides spending millions of dollars a year, they provide much-needed jobs for Kenyans, who work as guides, hotel employees, and entertainers. Kenya has what tourists like: friendly people, a beautiful countryside, and magnificent animals.

A Country That Sits on the Equator

Kenya is slightly smaller in area than the state of Texas. The equator passes through the middle of the country, which lies on the east coast of Africa. Its neighbors include Ethiopia and the Sudan to the north, Somalia to the east, Tanzania to the south, and Uganda to the west. In the southwest corner is Lake Victoria, the second-largest freshwater lake in the world. The Indian Ocean lies 300 miles (483 kilometers) along the country's eastern coast.

There are six geographic regions in Kenya: (1) the coastal lowlands; (2) the eastern plains; (3) the eastern and western highlands; (4) the Great Rift Valley; (5) the northern plateau; and (6) the western plateau.

From the Lowlands to the Highlands

A narrow strip of land makes up the coastal lowlands. Many beautiful beaches provide relief from the hot and humid climate. So do the winds that blow in from the ocean. As in most tropical climates, life here is slow paced. People don't worry about getting things done right away. If they don't find time today, tomorrow is just fine.

The land climbs gently from the coastal lowlands and becomes the eastern plains. This is savannah country: wide grasslands, scattered thorn trees, and rocky soil. A lot of animals live here but not many people. It is home to the world's tallest (giraffe) and fastest (cheetah) animals and the largest bird (ostrich). The savannah can be hot, and ostriches use their wings as umbrellas to shade their chicks. Giraffes nibble on high branches, while gazelles and impala munch on grasses and twigs closer to the ground.

By the time the eastern plains reach the highlands, the land has climbed 3,000 feet (914 meters). The region is divided by the Rift Valley into the eastern and western highlands. Kenya's capital and largest city, Nairobi, is in the eastern highlands. So is Mount Kenya, its highest mountain. This great mountain was originally called Kere-Nyaga (Mountain of Whiteness) by the Kikuyu people, who live in the area. In 1849, a European missionary saw the mountain and mispronounced the Kikuyu word as "Kenya." The country and the mountain have been known as Kenya ever since. Mount Kenya was once an active volcano. Before it blew its top, it was higher than Mount Everest, the world's tallest mountain. Even though Mount Kenya is on the equator, its twin peaks are covered with snow all year because it is so high (17,058 feet, or 5,199 meters).

The highlands are Kenya's best agricultural region. The rich soil, plentiful rainfall (40 inches, or 102 centimeters, a year), and mild climate are ideal for farming. The high altitude is perfect for coffee and tea production. Kenya is the world's third-largest tea producer, after India and Sri Lanka. The town of Kericho, in the western highlands, is the center of one of the most fertile tea-growing areas in the world. Tea is raised on large estates as well as on thousands of small plots of land owned by Kenyan farmers.

Turning so much of the highlands into farmland has been both good and bad for Kenyans. Farming provides jobs for many Kenyan workers. Exporting crops such as tea and coffee brings money into the country. But trees were chopped down to make the farms. Many of the

Workers harvest tea on a small farm in the highlands.

trees were part of the African rain forest, which once spread across the continent. Now only a fragment of rain forest, so important to the world's environment, is left in Kenya. Also, much of the wildlife has been forced out of the highlands because so many people live there.

A Slash in the Earth

The Great Rift Valley is a huge slash in the earth's surface. It is so vast that astronauts can see it on their space flights. The Rift runs for more than 5,400 miles (8,694 kilometers), from Syria in the Middle East to Mozambique in southeastern Africa. Many years ago, earthquakes and volcanic eruptions formed the valley and the two mountain chains that run along each side of it. On the west is the Mau Escarpment. (An escarpment is a steep cliff.) The Mau Escarpment is more than 9,800 feet (2,987 meters) above sea level and stretches 200 miles (322 kilometers) north from the Tanzania border. On the eastern side of the Great Rift is the Aberdare Range. These mountains are more than 13,000 feet (3,962 meters) high in places. Beyond each of these mountain chains lie the highlands.

The Great Rift Valley runs from 10 to 40 miles (16 to 64 kilometers) wide and in some places is nearly 3,000 feet (914 meters) deep. It has been called the "cradle of mankind" because the bones of our ancient ancestors have been found there. The many earthquakes along the Rift bring old bones up to the surface, where people can find them.

The most exciting of these discoveries have been made along the shores of Lake Turkana, the most northern of a chain of Rift Valley lakes. In 1972, a young

Kenyan named Bernard Ng'eneo walked through a gully and saw the tiny fragment of a skull. Anthropologist Richard Leakey and his helpers later found more than 300 pieces of the skull and reconstructed it. The skull is the earliest evidence of man's evolution from the ape. Richard Leakey's team is still excavating, or digging, the site, named Koobi Fora, to understand more about our origins.

Lake Turkana is the largest alkaline lake in the world. An alkaline lake is one so filled with minerals that most sea life cannot survive in it. When there are few fish in the water, bacteria and algae thrive. This is the main food for pink flamingos, and millions of these birds feed on the alkaline lakes in the Great Rift Valley.

Home of the Aardwolf

The northern plateau covers more than one-third of Kenya's land area but is a place where few Kenyans live. Less than 10 inches (25 centimeters) of rain falls each year, and only scrubby shrubs and scattered patches of grass can grow in this parched land. Nomads wander through this desert area searching for grazing land and water for their camels, goats, and sheep. They usually travel early in the morning and late in the afternoon to avoid the scorching midday sun.

Giraffes pause before they dip into the river for a drink.

A welcome oasis in the middle of the northern plateau is Mount Marsabit, an extinct volcano. It rises 5,585 feet (1,702 meters) above the barren land and captures most of the moisture in the air. Fine mists, formed from the moisture, wrap around the thick forests that grow along the sides of the mountain. These are perfect conditions for elephants, water buffaloes, and greater kudus. Giraffes, leopards, and aardwolves are other animals that live in the mist forests.

Gigantic Fish in a Big Lake

The western plateau slopes gently down to the Lake Victoria basin. Kenya's sugar cane production is centered here. The area gets as much as 60 inches (152 centimeters) of rain a year, and the climate is hot and humid. Lake Victoria, at 26,500 square miles (68,635 square kilometers), is Africa's largest lake. In the 1960s, big fish called Nile perch were brought to the lake. These fish eat everything! Now many species of smaller fish native to Lake Victoria have died out, or become extinct. Some Nile perch weigh as much as 397 pounds (179 kilograms)! To catch them, fishermen can no longer use nets made with natural fibers. Instead they buy synthetic fish line, the only material strong enough to catch these big fish.

Part of the western plateau is a savannah. The Mara

Plain is home to thousands of wild animals, as well as to descendants of the famous Masai warriors. The Masai now tend their livestock on the plains, still wearing colorful red robes. At night they herd the cattle into the middle of a circle of huts where they live. A thorn fence surrounds the huts and protects both the Masai and their livestock from wild animals.

A Moderate Climate in the Tropics

Although Kenya is on the equator, most of the country has a moderate climate because of the high altitudes. But in the low deserts of the north, temperatures sometimes reach 135°F (57°C). Along the coastal lowlands, temperatures average 80°F (27°C), but winds blowing across the Indian Ocean carry cooling breezes. These winds, called the northeast (kaskazi) and southeast (kusi) monsoons, determine the seasons. The warm kaskazi blows toward Kenya from the northeast between the months of October and March. The cooler kusi blows in from the southeast from April to September.

Kenya has two rainy seasons and two dry seasons. The northeast monsoon brings rain from October to December. These are called the short rains because it doesn't rain all day. There are a few hours of sunshine, usually in the late afternoon. During the southeast-monsoon months from April to early June, rain pours out of the sky all day, day after day. These are called the long rains, and the weather is much cooler. Light rain showers fall now and then throughout the dry seasons everywhere but in the northern region.

Growing Cities

Nairobi, Kenya's capital, is the fastest-growing city in Africa. More than a million people live in the city now, and by the year 2000, three to four million people are expected to reside there. For a number of reasons, more and more young Kenyans are moving to Nairobi from the countryside. Irrigation projects have turned some of the drier parts of the country into farmland, which leaves fewer areas for herdsmen to graze their livestock. Fewer cattle, sheep, and goats can be raised, so the children of herdsmen need to find other ways to make a living when they grow up. In the rich farmlands of the highlands, there is not enough land for fathers to give to each of their sons, so many young men go to Nairobi to look for work. Some young people want to live a more modern life, and so they move to Nairobi.

Nairobi is a truly international city. Africans, Asians, Europeans, and Americans live and do business there. Life is fast paced. The streets are crowded and colorful.

East Indians wearing turbans or saris can be seen bustling into government buildings alongside businessmen in Western suits. Tourists in safari outfits mingle with Kenyans dressed in colorful native clothes.

In the middle of the city is a 44-square-mile (114-square-kilometer) park populated by wild animals. They usually stay within the grasslands of the park, but every so often, an animal roams into the suburbs. Once a giraffe stepped into a manhole. Another time, a home owner found a leopard in his garden. In 1980, a few lions ate a cow and some horses. This doesn't happen often, and most Kenyans enjoy having animals all around them.

Mombasa is Kenya's second-largest city and its main port on the Indian Ocean. Ships have been sailing into and out of it for 2,000 years. In previous centuries, traders from the Middle East and as far away as China stopped at Mombasa. It was also a market for the slave trade.

Today, Mombasa is still important as a trading center. Kenya is the world's largest producer of pyrethrum, an insecticide made from dried chrysanthemum heads. The country also exports coffee, tea, pineapple, and trona. Trona, or soda ash, is a mineral found in the alkaline lakes of the Great Rift Valley. It is refined to make glass and detergents. Kenya imports crude oil, which it

Nairobi — the capital of Kenya and Africa's fastest-growing city.

processes in a refinery north of Mombasa and then ships all over East Africa. African countries without a seaport, such as Rwanda and Zaire, ship products through Mombasa also.

The third-largest city in Kenya is Kisumu. Located on the northeast corner of Lake Victoria, it is an important port. It is also the principal town in the western plateau region. Before roads were built in central Africa, Kisumu was the rail center for products shipped from Mombasa to Uganda, northern Tanzania, and Zaire.

Wanted: More Democracy

In 1963, Kenya became an independent republic. Its constitution was patterned after the U.S. constitution. Kenya has an executive branch (the president), a legislative branch (the National Assembly), and a separate judicial branch. In the United States, this setup provides for a system of checks and balances, so that no branch can become too powerful. The Kenyan government has not turned out this way. Most of the power belongs to the president.

The president is elected for a five-year term, and he can serve for an unlimited number of terms. Since gaining its independence, Kenya has had only two presidents: Jomo Kenyatta served for 14 years, and Daniel

A group of children in the ancient port city of Mombasa.

arap Moi has held the office since 1978. Since 1982, only one political party has been allowed in Kenya, and only one presidential candidate, so running for president has been no contest at all.

The National Assembly is made up of 170 members. Most of them — 158 — are elected for five-year terms, and the president appoints the other 12. He also selects Kenya's vice president from among the members of the National Assembly. Voters elect assembly members from a list of candidates approved by KANU (Kenya African National Union), Kenya's sole political party. This is more of a contest than the presidential election, since several candidates usually run for each seat.

President Moi likes to call Kenya's system of government a democracy, but that's not true. He has banned opposition parties. In fact, only recently, in December 1991, has he promised to allow a multiparty system. Government censorship of the news is common. Kenyans are afraid to criticize government policies for fear of ending up in jail. Sometimes a person's human rights are violated. One such violation is when a person is imprisoned without being charged with a crime and is held without a trial for months at a time.

Kenya's government does have its good points. It is one of the most stable governments in Africa. There has never been a civil war, and Kenya has escaped the chaos that many of its neighbors have suffered. It is one of the most modern countries in all of Africa and the most prosperous in East Africa. If the checks and balances originally planned for their constitution could be put into place, Kenyans could have a democratic government.

2. *From* Uhuru *to* Harambee

"*Uhuru*," shouted Jomo Kenyatta as he led his fellow Kenyans in their struggle against the British, who had run the government of Kenya since 1895. "Uhuru" is the Swahili word for "freedom." Kenyatta began his campaign to make Kenya an independent country, rather than a British colony, in 1924. He did not succeed until December 12, 1963.

Then he began another campaign called *harambee,* which means "let's pull together" in Swahili. Kenyans come from more than 40 different tribes, now often called ethnic groups. Some groups have been great rivals. Others never had much to do with one another. If the ethnic groups didn't pull together, Kenyatta feared the country would fall apart, and outsiders could step in to govern Kenya again.

Although the various ethnic groups in Kenya are pulling together for the good of the country, they still keep in touch with their tribal past. This is often expressed in music and dance. The herders celebrate the onset of the rainy season by singing together. Others play ancient tunes on reed flutes and sing the songs of their forefathers. Young children learn their ancestral songs and sing them the rest of their lives.

Dancing has always been important to Kenyans. Just as they sing together, they dance together. Men do line dances, and some groups compete to see who can jump the highest during the dance. Women dance with other women, following the rhythm of the songs they are singing. Children learn these dances as they take part in such ceremonies as marriage, the naming of a child, and initiation rites, which is when boys and girls take on the responsibilities of adult life (between the ages of 12 and 15).

Another way children learn about their traditions is by listening to stories. Storytellers are thought of as artists. Anyone who can tell the myths, folktales, and legends of a culture is highly respected. Before Kenyans had a written language, they learned history by listening to the storytellers. This is called oral history.

The Kikuyu and the Luyha

Kenya is a melting pot of ethnic groups, even more so than the United States. Each ethnic group has its own language, traditional beliefs, and culture. A Kikuyu feels as different from a Turkana as a native New Yorker does from someone who has lived all his life in the hills of Kentucky. A Luo from the Lake Victoria region has very

Young girls of the Samburu tribe. Although some Samburu have left their homeland for the cities, many remain herders and follow the nomadic ways of their ancestors.

little in common with a Giriama, who lives along the Indian Ocean, although both are traditionally fishermen.

The Kikuyu form the largest ethnic group in Kenya. Many live on *shambas,* or small farms, in the fertile high-

lands near Mount Kenya. They are hard-working farmers who produce nearly all of the fruits and vegetables for Nairobi. They also grow coffee; sisal, a fiber from which strong rope is made; and pyrethrum for export.

The most famous Kikuyu was Jomo Kenyatta, Kenya's first president. He stressed the importance of education in building a better country. Ever since, Kikuyu parents have spent much of the money they earn on their children's education. They expect them to excel in school so they can become successful citizens. Today, many are lawyers, accountants, teachers, doctors, and businessmen. Some have become active in national politics, and many have held high government positions.

The Luyha, who make up Kenya's second-largest ethnic group, have also been involved in politics, and like the Kikuyu, they are rapidly educating their children. They farm small plots of land on the slopes of Mount Elgon, in western Kenya, but their area is so crowded that many have moved to nearby towns and Nairobi to work.

The Luo and the Kalenjin

The third-largest group is the Luo, who live in the Lake Victoria basin and along its shores. Some are expert fishermen and boat-builders. Others are farmers, growing maize — a kind of corn — rice, cotton, and sugar cane. Like the Kikuyu and the Luhya, the Luo are influential in Kenya's government. Many Luo have moved to nearby Kisumu or farther away to Nairobi or Mombasa. There they are skilled mechanics and craftsmen and dominate Kenyan trade unions.

The Kalenjin, who make up Kenya's fourth-largest group, live in the western highlands and on the higher slopes of the western Rift Valley. Kalenjin is the general name given to a group of related peoples who share many of the same traditions and speak dialects of the same language. The most famous Kalenjin is President Daniel arap Moi, who belongs to the Tugen subgroup. Other subgroups include the Kipsigis, Nandi, Marakwet, and Pokot. Much of Kenya's tea is raised in Kalenjin country, and many of the country's famous runners have come from this area.

In the early 1900s, when the British were building their railroad into western Kenya, Nandi warriors fiercely fought them. The Nandi also stole the iron rails and made them into spear points. They removed copper telegraph wire to use for jewelry. The British forces finally defeated the Nandi, drove them into a native reserve, and took over their land for white settlers.

The Turkana

Nomadic herdsmen in Kenya's dry north live much as their ancestors always have. Twentieth-century life has barely touched them, although the government is developing irrigation projects that will change that.

The Turkana homeland is around Lake Turkana. Crocodiles bask at the edge of the water under the hot

sun and sometimes provide a tasty meal for these people. Occasionally, a crocodile makes a meal of a care-
less Turkana who gets too close to its snapping jaws.

Life revolves around the Turkana's camels, cattle,
goats, sheep, and donkeys. The larger a family's herds, the
more it is respected. Boys and girls begin herding sheep
and goats when they are about eight years old. Older boys
leave the family homestead, called an *awi*, to join the men
herding the camels and cattle in the desert scrub.

Older girls stay in the awi to help make the huts,
sleeping mats, and sandals. When they finish their
chores, they make jewelry. Turkana women and girls
wear so many layers of bead necklaces that their long
necks are covered to their bare chests. Beads come from
natural materials. The glossy black and brown seeds of
the acacia tree and the bones of fish or snakes are strung
into necklaces. Ostrich eggshells are sliced into disks,
strung, and worn in layers high on the neck. They look
like zebra stripes. Young women also sew these disks on
their clothing to show that they are unmarried. They
wear fish bones as good-luck symbols — in hopes of
having many children.

The Turkana homestead includes a man, his wife or
wives, and their children. His married sons and their
children also live in the awi. When a girl marries, she
leaves her family and moves to the awi of her husband.
It is the custom for a Turkana husband to pay for his

The Turkana people live in Kenya's dry north. Huts like this one are built by women and the older girls of the tribe.

bride. This "bride price," as it is called, could be as much as 50 cows and 100 or more goats. The groom gets the animals from his own and his father's herds and sometimes from the herds of his mother's brothers.

The Rendille

Bride price for the Rendille is paid in camels. While cattle are of great value to these nomads, camels are more

important. Camels give two to three times more milk than
cows do. Milk mixed with blood is the main diet of these
and many other Kenyan nomads. Blood provides the pro-
tein they need, since they don't eat much meat. A knife or
sharp arrow is used to cut into a vein in the camel's
throat. (This doesn't hurt the animal.) After a small
amount of blood is drained into a hollow gourd, the
wound is closed with a mixture of hair and camel dung.

The Rendille live in semipermanent settlements in
the northern desert country, south of the Turkana. Married men, women, and children stay in the settlements.
Older boys and young men herd the camels and cattle
across the desert, setting up camps wherever they find
enough grass for their animals. Everyone celebrates
after the rainy season because there is good grazing for
the animals close to the settlements and families can be
together.

Finding water is a major occupation for these desert
people. While young girls tend the herds of sheep and
goats, it is the job of the women in the settlement to
fetch water. Sometimes they walk as far as 36 miles (58
kilometers) a day to find water in this dry land. Rendille
men are known for their singing wells. They dig wells
by hand many feet deep to locate water. They then form
bucket brigades from the wells to their thirsty animals.
As they pass the leather buckets from one man to the
next, they chant their ancestral songs.

Herders and Safari Guides

The tall, lean figures of Samburu and Masai herders stand out against the thornbush scrubland. They wrap themselves in pieces of red cloth, either tied around the waist or over one shoulder, and they carry long spears. Many stick to the nomadic way of their forefathers, although modern life is intruding into their cultures. Some of the young men have migrated to urban areas to find work.

A number of Masai have completed school and have become businessmen and doctors. Some Masai have gotten jobs in Nairobi as night watchmen because of their reputation for being courageous warriors.

Many Samburu have become policemen or soldiers in the Kenyan army. Other Samburu and Masai stay closer to their homelands, employed as rangers or safari guides in the game parks. Tourists come from all over the world to take a safari, or journey, through Kenya's famous game parks to see the wildlife.

The Samburu

The Samburu are related to the Masai, although each group lives in a different area of Kenya. The Samburu live just above the equator, where the foothills of Mount Kenya merge into the northern desert. A ribbon of green trees cuts through Samburu country along the banks of the Uasox Nyiro River. Crocodiles and hippopotamuses live in the brown waters, and chattering monkeys scramble through the trees.

The Samburu are a friendly people. They have learned their tribal history from storytellers, and they like nothing better than to tell their stories to anyone who will listen.

Like their Turkana and Rendille neighbors, the Samburu center their lives around their cows, camels, goats, and sheep. Milk is their main food, sometimes mixed with blood. They make soups from certain roots and barks, and those who live in upland areas grow vegetables to add to their diet. Meat is eaten only on special occasions.

The birth of a baby is celebrated by killing a sheep for a feast. Graduation ceremonies are also occasions for feasting and merrymaking. The Samburu (and the Masai) follow an interesting tradition as people go through the stages of their lives. Boys and girls are organized into groups, called age-sets. Each age-set includes all the children born during a three- or four-year period. Instead of celebrating individual birthdays, the Samburu go through a series of ceremonies with others in their age-set.

Samburu children have a graduation ceremony — or

Samburu warriors hold competitions
to see who can jump the highest.

initiation rite — when girls are around 12 years old and boys a little older. For some time prior to this ceremony, they study their tribal traditions and prepare to become responsible adults. After their initiation ceremonies, the young Samburu leave their childhood behind and become members of the adult community. The girls can marry after this ceremony and most do, usually between the ages of 12 and 15. The boys do not marry for at least 11 years.

Following their initiation ceremony, the boys become *murrani,* or junior warriors. Five years later, the members of the age-set go through another ceremony to become senior warriors. During these years, they are responsible for taking care of their community. They herd the cattle to good grazing areas, sometimes driving the animals hundreds of miles before they find enough grass. The boys always carry a herding stick in one hand and a spear in the other, in case a lion attacks them or their cattle.

Samburu girls flirt with the young warriors, hoping to become "beaded" by their favorite. If a warrior likes a girl, he buys layer after layer of necklaces for her. Samburu men carry their money in old socks that hang knotted around their belts. Before they marry, they each have to pay a bride price, but they do not use the money in their socks. Instead, they give each bride's family a certain number of cattle and sheep.

The Mighty Masai

When people think about Kenya, they usually picture a tall, athletic Masai, holding a long spear and a shield of decorated buffalo hide. The Masai are known for their great courage, and their warlike reputation has made them both respected and feared by other Kenyans. The Masai believe that, in the beginning, their legendary god, Ngai, gave all the world's cattle to them. In fact, they used to steal cattle from neighboring tribes. That is now against the law in Kenya, although the Masai have been known to cross the border into Tanzania and steal a few cattle. They believe they are merely taking back what Ngai says belongs to them.

They love their cattle the way they love their children, and often sing to the animals. They tell them where to go by whistling them along. Whistles have meanings: The cattle know whether to move to the left or right, if there is water nearby, or when they are going home.

The wealth of the Masai is measured by the number of cattle and children they have. A modestly wealthy Masai has 50 head of cattle plus children. Some Masai have as many as a 1,000 cattle in one herd. But if they have no children, they are not considered wealthy. Cattle and children are the most important treasures in a Masai's life.

Masai territory extends across west-central Kenya

Masai women and girls gather to sell jewelry they have made.

on both sides of the Kenya–Tanzania border. Their lands used to be much larger. In the early 1900s, the white settlers took over the rich Masai pasturelands and pushed the people south onto reserves one-fifth the size of their old lands. Later, the government took away more of their lands for two wildlife parks: Amboseli National Park in the east and Masai Mara in the west. Today their territory continues to shrink, as more and more of their pastureland is being turned into farmland to feed the nation's growing population.

Many Masai now lead a double life: half modern and half traditional. They may wear cutoff jeans instead of a red cloth tied over one shoulder, and sometimes they may even use a digital watch. But they continue to learn the traditions of their people and are proud to be Masai.

Europeans, Asians, and Arabs

Most Kenyans — 98 percent — are black Africans. The remaining 2 percent are of European, Asian, or Arab background. The Europeans first came as missionaries, traders, and farmers in the 1800s and early 1900s. The Leakey family is probably the best known of the Europeans. Louis Leakey, the son of British missionaries, grew up with the Kikuyu. He and his wife, Mary, were anthropologists who made important discoveries about the origins of man. Their son Richard continues their work. Their younger son, Philip, is the only white member of Kenya's National Assembly.

Joy and George Adamson, also Europeans, are well-known for having saved orphaned wildlife at their savannah camp. After taking the young animals in, the Adamsons would train them to fend for themselves so that they could return to the wild. Joy Adamson wrote two best-selling books in the 1960s about the animals they raised, *Born Free* and *Living Free.*

Asians from India and Pakistan came to Kenya in the

1890s as railroad workers and traders. They settled in the cities and towns and earned their living as clerks in banks, post offices, and businesses. Many became merchants. Some set up little shops called *dukas* all over Kenya and became quite successful. Native Kenyans were jealous of their success, and anti-Asian feelings arose. In 1967 Jomo Kenyatta said that all foreigners needed work permits for jobs Kenyans could do. Many Asians were forced to leave the country — even those who had been born in Kenya and considered it their home. Today, only about 80,000 Asians remain in the country.

Arab traders from the Arabian peninsula arrived in the 700s, looking for ivory, slaves, and animal skins. Some settled along the coast and intermarried with the local people. The Swahili culture developed from this union of Arabs and Africans. Today, their lives center around their Muslim faith. At sundown, men gather near the mosques — Muslim places of worship — waiting for the call to prayer. Women dress in the black *chador,* which covers them from head to toe. Men wear the *kanzu,* a full-length white robe, and a red cap, called a *kofia.* Today most Arabs who live on the coast are merchants. Those who live inland work on coconut plantations.

These young Swahili women, who live along the coast, wear the chador — *a sign that they belong to the Muslim faith.*

3. *Cradle of Mankind*

About 25 million years ago, Kenya was a lushly forested plateau that sloped toward the Indian Ocean. Apes, which scientists believe were the ancestors of man, lived peacefully in the forests. Their quiet way of life was disturbed when the plateau rose in the shape of a dome and molten rock burst through the surface, forming huge volcanoes. Then the dome began to crack from north to south. The crack became wider over millions of years as a series of earthquakes formed the Great Rift Valley.

Streams flowed into the lowest parts of the valley, forming a chain of lakes on the valley floor. Eventually, some of the ape families moved from the forests into the grasslands of the Great Rift Valley, where they lived on the shores of the lakes. Scientists believe that three to four million years ago, one or more of the ape families began evolving into man's earliest ancestors, sometimes called protohumans. ("Proto" means the earliest form of something.) The campsites, stone tools, and bones of these protohumans were covered by sand from rising lake water and by deposits of ash from constantly erupting volcanoes.

Lake Nakuru, one of the chain of lakes in the Great Rift Valley.

Their remains were buried until the early 1960s, when Louis and Mary Leakey found protohuman fossils while digging in the Great Rift Valley. Earthquakes, which continue to shake up the soil in the Great Rift Valley, have brought fossils and bones fairly close to the surface. In 1972, Richard Leakey dug up parts of a human skull thought to be 2.2 million years old. In 1984, on the shores of Lake Turkana, he dug up the almost complete skeleton of a 12-year-old male, a predecessor of modern man.

Thousands of years ago, an ancient people wandered around the high plateau of East Africa, hunting wildlife such as hippopotamus and gathering roots and berries. Later, when they learned how to tame animals, some of them became herders of cattle, goats, sheep, and camels. They roamed the wide grasslands with their herds in search of food for their animals. Some of these herders learned how to cultivate the land and settled down to farm the more fertile highland areas. Others stayed on the grasslands with their herds.

Newcomers . . . and the Slave Trade

People from other parts of the continent began migrating to East Africa around A.D. 500. They were seeking fertile farmland and pastures for their animals. Sometimes the newcomers intermarried with those who were already living there. Other times, they pushed them out of the area. Bantu-speaking people from central Africa migrated to East Africa. Other groups came from the Nile River Valley and from Ethiopia. These peoples belonged to a variety of ethnic groups. Each had its own language, customs, and religion. This accounts for the many ethnic groups living in Kenya today.

While these groups were settling the interior of Kenya, other people were sailing along the coast. They were traders from Arabia, Persia (the former name for Iran), and southwest Asia. Most of these traders were Arabs, who brought the Muslim religion to Africa. The Arabs settled mainly in the coastal towns and intermarried with the local people. A need naturally arose for one language that everyone could understand. Thus Swahili developed. Swahili is a mixture of Bantu — a group of widely used African languages — and Arabic. Today, Swahili and English are Kenya's national languages.

The coastal cities thrived for several hundred years. Then European countries became interested in Kenya's money-making trade and fertile soil. The Portuguese came first. In the 1480s, Vasco da Gama sailed around the southern tip of Africa, searching for a sea route to India. Unfriendly Arabs greeted his arrival in Mombasa. They feared competition from the Europeans for the trade that had made the coastal towns rich. The Arabs' fears were not unfounded. Da Gama later told other Portuguese explorers about the wealthy trading centers. The Portuguese sent warships and attacked the coastal towns. For the next 250 years, the Portuguese and Arabs fought a series of battles along the coast of East Africa. Finally the Arabs defeated the Portuguese, who left that part of Africa forever.

The Arabs continued to trade. They exchanged ivory and rhinoceros horns for silks and other luxuries from China. They also set up a profitable business in slavery. At first they captured slaves from the Kenyan coast. By the 1860s, however, they had begun searching the interior, and a slave trail ran all the way to Lake Victoria. At the peak of the slave trade in East Africa, 25,000 slaves a year were sold to Persia, Arabia, and India.

Christian missionaries from Europe arrived in the mid-1800s and began speaking out against slavery. Great Britain had abolished slavery in England in 1807, and the British pressured the Arabs to end their slave trade. But that did not happen until 1873, when the sultan of Zanzibar signed a treaty with the British, putting an end to the selling of slaves on the east coast of Africa.

British Domination

Great Britain and other European countries realized the importance of Africa in the mid-to-late 1800s. They saw that the continent could provide them with natural resources and such products as coffee, tea, and cotton. There was intense competition among the Western powers for trade and influence. Settlers were encouraged to

Nairobi in the early 1900s, under the rule of the British.

form colonies in Africa. Before long, Britain and other European countries ruled nearly all of the great continent. The natives' spears and bows and arrows were no match for European guns.

Britain controlled what is today Kenya, Uganda, and a portion of Somalia. The territory became part of the British Empire. Declaring Kenya a colony meant that British citizens could take the land and natural resources for themselves. To make it easier for settlers to get to the interior of the country, the government built a railroad. It ran for more than 600 miles (966 kilometers), from the port of Mombasa on the coast to Lake Victoria in the interior.

The railroad, begun in 1895, took six years to complete. Thousands of workers were brought from India to help build it, just as thousands of Chinese were brought to the United States to build its railroads. Africans were afraid to work in Masai territory because these fierce warriors raided everyone around them. Railroad workers had no trouble with the Masai, perhaps because the workers were protected by modern weapons. But they did have problems with malaria and wild animals. Lions killed 28 Indian workers. Africans believed that each time a lion ate a railroad worker, a dead chief had returned in the form of a lion to punish the worker for building "the iron snake," as they called the railroad.

The British and other European colonists set up farms on either side of the tracks. They forced native Kenyans off their ancestral lands. As more foreigners came to British East Africa, more Kenyans were pushed to less desirable farmland. Finally, in order to make enough fertile land available to all the settlers, Kenyans were forced onto the native reserves. This was similar to the way in which the United States government placed Native Americans in reservations in order to take over their lands.

The colonists developed large tea and coffee plantations. They needed laborers for their farms, but the Kenyans refused to work the land that had been taken from them. In response, the British colonial government passed laws requiring Kenyans to work on the settlers' farms, where they were paid low wages. Also, they were forbidden to grow coffee and other cash crops on their own farms. While European settlers prospered under these conditions, Africans grew poorer and more frustrated.

Although they were vastly outnumbered by native Kenyans and workers who had come from India, the British maintained their control. Only settlers could serve on the Legislative Council, which ruled the colony. Only settlers could vote on laws that affected the lives of all Kenyans.

Kenyans Rebel

During the 1920s, native Kenyans began to rebel against British domination. Many of those who had been pushed off their highland farms moved to the cities of Nairobi or Nakuru to look for jobs. Good jobs were difficult to find because Europeans refused to hire Kenyans for well-paying positions. Also, most Kenyans were not trained in modern technology and services. Life was tough in the cities, and native Kenyans met secretly to talk about their problems.

In Nairobi, Harry Thuku, a young leader of the Kikuyu people, formed the Kikuyu Association. He urged members not to work on settlers' farms and to destroy the hated identification cards the government required them to carry. Thuku's group was the first to rebel against British rule. In 1922, Thuku was arrested and banished to northern Kenya.

Other rebellious groups were formed, and members held mass meetings to complain about British domination. One of the Kenyans who enthusiastically participated in these meetings was another young Kikuyu, Jomo Kenyatta. In 1928, he quit his job reading water meters to enter politics full time. He became a spokesman for African land and civil rights. He even went to London to try to talk the British Parliament into allowing native Kenyans to be elected to the Legislative Council. He asked again and again, but Parliament kept turning him down.

Meanwhile, the workers from India who had settled in Kenya were doing better. In 1923, they were granted five seats on the Legislative Council. The settlers had eleven seats. Native Kenyans were represented by only one white European missionary.

Finally, in 1944, the British appointed a native Kenyan to the Legislative Council. But Kenyans wanted to choose their own representative. And they wanted more than one. They wanted majority rule. Since there were more native Kenyans than settlers in the colony, the majority of representatives on the Legislative Council should, they believed, be Kenyans. They formed the Kenya African Union (KAU) and chose Kenyatta as its leader. The KAU supported a series of strikes throughout the country to demonstrate opposition to British rule. The government ruthlessly put down the strikes. Kenyans retaliated with acts of violence against the settlers, and the British colonial government jailed thousands of them.

The Mau Mau Rebellion

In 1952, the Mau Mau Rebellion erupted. The Mau Mau was a secret society formed by Kikuyus who resented British rule. The Mau Mau became a guerrilla army, fighting for land and freedom. They lived in the highland forests near Nairobi and attacked at night. They destroyed settlers' farms, sometimes killing the colonists, their wives, and their children. They also murdered Kenyans who were loyal to the colonial government. In response, the police killed many innocent Africans and forced Kikuyus off their farms and shipped them to reserves.

In October 1952, government officials declared a state of emergency. Although Kenyatta had condemned the violence and had urged everyone to work toward peaceful change, he was accused of leading the uprising. He was arrested and sentenced to seven years of hard labor in a remote part of Kenya.

Kenyatta's arrest angered native Kenyans and brought them closer together. The violence increased rather than decreased. The British then began to listen to Kenyan demands. By 1959, the British realized that their domination could not continue. In 1960, Great Britain granted Kenyans majority rule and eventual independence.

Two political parties formed, the Kenya African National Union (KANU) and the Kenya African Democratic Union (KADU). Even though Kenyatta was still in prison, he was elected leader of the KANU. He had completed his sentence, but the British governor had refused to release him, for fear that greater violence would break out. In February 1961, elections were held to choose members for Kenya's new parliament. The KANU party won a majority of the seats but refused to take office until Kenyatta was released. Finally, on August 15, 1961, Kenyatta became a free man.

Uhuru

On December 12, 1963, Great Britain granted Kenya full independence. Kenyans gathered in city streets and rural villages shouting *"Uhuru!"*("Freedom!") The

Jomo Kenyatta speaking at the opening of a United Nations office in Nairobi shortly before Kenya was granted independence.

British flag was lowered, and the black, red, and green flag of the new Kenyan republic was raised throughout the country. The flag is a symbol of Kenya's struggle for independence. The black horizontal stripe stands for Kenyans; the red stripe, their struggle for freedom; and the green stripe, their agricultural lands. Two narrow white stripes symbolize peace and unity. The Masai war shield in front of crossed spears represents the defense of freedom.

Jomo Kenyatta became Kenya's first president. The KADU party dissolved and joined the KANU, and Kenya became a one-party nation. In 1966, a new party, called Kenya's Peoples Union (KPU), was formed. President Kenyatta outlawed the KPU three years later, however, accusing the party's leaders of antigovernment activities. Since then, Kenya has been a one-party state under the rule of one man.

Kenyatta was a notable leader. He united the different ethnic groups by promoting his policy of harambee, or "pulling together." His government acquired settler farms and sold or rented the land to native Kenyans. He did not allow communist activities within Kenya, although he tried to stay friends with communist countries as well as with Western capitalist countries. Under Kenyatta's unquestioned leadership, Kenya became the most politically stable country on the African continent.

In 1973, Kenya celebrated ten years of independence. Kenyans were pleased with the achievements under Kenyatta's rule. Education was free to everyone for the first four years. More children were going to school than ever before. The national income had doubled, tea production had tripled, and coffee production had increased by 50 percent. Many North American companies invested in Kenya. This was good for Kenyans because foreign business provided jobs.

A New President

Jomo Kenyatta died in 1978, when he was 86 years old. The constitution provided for the vice president, Daniel arap Moi, to become president. An election held a few months later made Moi the official president of Kenya, and he has held the job ever since. Kenyans were pleased at the beginning of his rule, when he released 26 political prisoners and promised Kenyans more freedom. But Kenya's economy did not improve the way it had under Kenyatta. Because of the country's huge population growth, there were not enough jobs or land, and people became dissatisfied.

The 1980s were difficult for Kenya. In 1981, a long drought resulted in a food shortage. Students criticized the government and marched in demonstrations against Moi's policies. Moi closed the university several times. There was also unrest among teachers in Kenya, and

even doctors went on strike. On August 1, 1982, law
and order broke down when a group of air force rebels
attempted a military coup, or overthrow of the government. University students demonstrated in support of
the coup, and slum dwellers looted shops in downtown
Nairobi. Moi's troops shot the looters, overcame the
rebels, and restored law and order.

Then Moi tightened his grip on the government.
When he heard about plans to create an opposition
party, he amended the constitution so that the KANU
was the only legal party. He cracked down further with
more constitutional amendments. The secret ballot was
eliminated in primary elections. Voters now have to line
up in public behind a picture of the candidate they wish
to vote for. Top-level judges, who previously had
remained in office for life, just as members of the U.S.
Supreme Court do, have had this right taken away. If
Moi does not like a judge's decisions, he dismisses him.
KANU party members who speak out against the government are expelled. Newspapers and magazines that
print articles critical of Moi's policies are shut down.

Moi's critics are demanding an end to Kenya's
one-party rule. They want their country to become a
multiparty democracy. But Moi believes a multiparty
system would lead to ethnic fighting. Some Kenyans
agree with him. They compare the chaos and poverty in
other parts of Africa, which are the result of tribal war-

fare, to the peace and prosperity Kenya has generally enjoyed since its independence. But in December 1991, Moi finally agreed to allow other political parties to form. Western democracies threatened to cut off economic aid if he did not.

While many people disapprove of President Moi's political policies, they praise him for the way in which he has handled Kenya's wildlife crisis. For a number of years, poachers had been killing the country's wildlife, primarily its elephants and rhinoceroses. (Poachers are people who hunt animals illegally.) Kenya's elephant herds decreased from 140,000 animals in 1970 to 16,000 in 1989. Its rhinoceros population declined from 20,000 to 500 in the same period.

Wildlife has been killed in Kenya for as long as people have been there, but only in small numbers and primarily for food. Poachers killed the elephants and rhinos, hacked off their tusks and horns, and left them to rot in the equatorial sun. Elephant tusks provide valuable ivory, and the rhinoceros horn is in great demand for its medicinal uses in the Orient and for dagger handles in the Middle East.

The animals were in danger of becoming extinct if something wasn't done. Moi appointed Richard Leakey director of Kenya Wildlife Services. Leakey immediately fired 2,000 game-park officials who were suspected of aiding or joining the poachers. He gave park

Thousands of magnificent elephants have been killed in Kenya for their ivory tusks.

rangers automatic rifles and helicopter gunships to fight the poachers. Some 2,500 elephant tusks were taken from the poachers and dumped in a 15-foot-high heap. Then President Moi burned them in a huge bonfire.

They could have brought more than $3 million on the international ivory market.

Perhaps the greatest problems Kenya faces in the 1990s is its soaring birth rate. With so many people, there is neither enough land to farm nor enough jobs for those who go to the cities seeking work. Family planning clinics have been set up throughout the country to encourage Kenyans to limit the number of children they have.

For nearly 30 years, Kenya has been one of the most stable countries in Africa. If the country can control its population growth and develop more jobs, and if President Moi pushes forward with democratic reforms, then Kenya can continue to be a model for other African nations.

4. Stories Old and New

Kenyans love a good story, and there are many stories to tell. Each ethnic group has its own legends and myths that have been passed from one generation to the next since ancient times. Children gather after dinner in the home of the best storyteller in their village, usually a grandmother. She tells them tales she remembers from her childhood. Since everyone has heard the stories before, she must make them interesting. She mimics each character in a different voice, and many times she asks the children to help by acting out parts of the story. Sometimes she sings a story, and the children respond by singing the chorus.

Some stories tell about tribal history. Often spirits are involved. Many Kenyans believe the spirits of family members who have died are still around, watching them. The first story in this chapter, "Never Ask Me about My Family," is an example of this kind of tale.

Other stories illustrate a tribe's values and its ideas of correct behavior. This is not as boring as it sounds, because often the characters in the stories are animals. Kenyan children love animal tales. "A Man Who Could Transform Himself" is such a story.

"Never Ask Me about My Family"

Long ago, a young man called Mwenendega went down to a river not far from his home. On the left bank of the river, he saw a beautiful girl. He spoke to her: "Kind and beautiful girl, how are you?"

"I am very well."

"Gracious girl, where is your home?"

"I have no father, no mother, and nowhere to stay."

"If that is the truth, would you agree to come with me and become my beloved wife?"

The girl looked pleased and answered in a sweet voice: "With great pleasure I consent, but on one essential condition, which is this: During all of our life, you must never ask me about my father, my mother, or my country of origin."

Mwenendega replied, "I will never ask about your father, your mother, or your country during all of our life."

And so they married, and there was a great celebration. All Mwenendega's relatives came, and there was dancing and singing and a great feast.

Many happy years passed, and seven children were born to Mwenendega and his beloved wife. The children grew and the time arrived for the firstborn to have his coming-of-age ceremony. Near the end of the solemn rituals, just before each of the initiates shaved the hair

Like people everywhere, Kenyans love a good story.

from his head, Mwenendega said to his beloved wife: "Darling, from the day of our marriage until now, I have never seen your father or your mother. What has prevented them from coming today to see their grandchildren, how fine and strong they are? Don't you think that they should have taken part in this family feast?"

At the sound of those words, his wife grew frantic. She rose from the ground like a bouncing ball and fell down heavily on the earth, making a hole seven miles deep. At the same time, stones, trees, rubble, and mud shot into the air, like a blast of gunpowder. She shouted with an awful cry, "My father, my mother, and all my kinfolk, where are they? Children of Mboto, come out."

After her cry, the old spirits came down from the top of Mount Kenya. The people in Mwenendega's village heard a horn and the loud tom-tom of a beating drum. There was a great noise in the air and on the earth, and a hailstorm covered the ground with iced stones. Thunder rumbled loudly in the sky, and lightning flashed from one end of the country to the other.

The terrified people of Mwenendega's village hid in their huts and in nearby caverns. The old spirits found Mwenendega and carried him and his wife and his children to the top of Mount Kenya, where they buried them in a big hole under the stones.

Since then, whenever the Kikuyu slaughter a goat

From one generation to the next, Kenyans pass down their ancient myths and legends.

or make a sacrifice of some kind, they glance up at Mount Kenya, lest some misfortune happen to them as it did to Mwenendega and his family.

"A Man Who Could Transform Himself"

Mbokothe and his brother were orphans. Their parents had left them two cows when they died. One day, Mbokothe told his brother he wanted to take the two cows to a medicine man to trade them for a treatment that would give him magical powers. His brother agreed that he could take the cows.

Mbokothe led the cows to a famous medicine man in another part of the country. The medicine man treated him and gave him magical powers so that he could transform himself into any kind of animal that he wanted. He returned home and told his brother about his magical powers.

One day, Mbokothe transformed himself into a huge bull, and his brother took him to the market. All the people wondered where such a big bull had come from. One man asked how much the bull cost. The brother told him he would exchange it for two cows and five goats. So the man bought the bull, thinking such a big bull would impress the father of the girl he wanted to marry.

The man led the bull toward his home, but before

they got there, the bull escaped and ran away. The man chased after it, but the bull transformed itself into a lion and disappeared into the forest. The man who was following the bull's trail saw on the ground the prints of a lion's paw. He exclaimed, "It has already been eaten by a lion."

When the lion was far from where people lived, it transformed itself back into a man, and Mbokothe returned home. He saw the cows and goats that his brother had obtained from the market that day.

On another market day, Mbokothe transformed himself into a bull again, and his brother sold him for ten goats. Unfortunately for Mbokothe and his brother, the man who bought the bull had also been to the medicine man and had gotten magical powers. When they came near the house of the man, the bull ran off, and the man chased it into the forest. Mbokothe transformed himself into a lion, thinking the man would be scared if he saw a lion. But the man also changed himself into a lion and continued to chase Mbokothe.

When Mbokothe was about to be caught, he changed himself into a bird and flew away. But the man changed himself into a hawk and chased the bird in the sky. When Mbokothe was on the point of being caught, he came down to the ground and changed himself into an antelope. The man changed himself into a wolf and

Animals — like this hyena — are often the main characters in Kenyan folktales.

continued to chase the antelope until Mbokothe turned himself into a man again. The wolf did the same.

Mbokothe knew he could not magically turn himself into any animal and get away from the man. So he told him, "Okay, let's go to my home and I'll give you back your ten goats."

They went, and Mbokothe gave him back his goats.

Proverbs

Like the ancient stories, Kenyan proverbs have been passed down orally for hundreds of years. Proverbs are short sayings that give a message or moral. Kenyan mothers and grandmothers use proverbs to teach children good behavior. Here are some examples:

He who receives a gift does not measure. (A gift should be valued, no matter how simple it is.)

It is the duty of children to wait on elders, not the elders on children. (Honor thy father and thy mother.)

A man who continually laments is not heeded. (No one listens to someone who complains all the time.)

Thunder is not yet rain. (Don't count your chickens until they're hatched.)

He who is unable to dance says that the yard is stony. (Don't make excuses for something you can't do.)

Swahili proverbs are woven into the *kanga,* a rectangular piece of cloth worn by coastal women and children. The proverb on one kanga reads "A good old woman is like a bunch of bananas." This means a good old woman has lots of children!

Modern Literature

In the 1960s, more Westerners began to read African literature. Jomo Kenyatta wrote a book in English called *Facing Mount Kenya.* He described Kenyan customs and life from the viewpoint of a native.

The American writer Ernest Hemingway told about his safari experiences in Kenya, where he saw animals in the wild that most Westerners had seen only in zoos. Joy Adamson, the Englishwoman who cared for orphaned wildlife, wrote about Elsa the lioness in *Born Free.* Baroness Karen Blixen-Finecke from Denmark wrote *Out of Africa,* which described the years she spent on a coffee farm near Nairobi. *Born Free* and *Out of Africa* were later made into movies.

Today, some Kenyans are writing books in tribal languages so that more Africans can read them, not only those who know English. The best known of these authors is Ngugi wa Thiong'o. His first plays and novels came out in English, but in 1977 he decided to write only in Swahili and Kikuyu. Ngugi had another purpose in mind when he switched to these languages. He wanted to criticize the Kenyan government. For this, he was arrested and put in jail.

When he got out a year later, he wrote another play in Kikuyu called *Mother Sing to Me.* Even poor people with no schooling could understand the play, which was about injustice and government corruption. In 1982, Ngugi had to flee to England to avoid being jailed again. He still lives there, unable to return home without losing his freedom.

5. Holidays and Festivals

Holidays are celebrated with a lot of enthusiasm in Kenya. There are 11 official holidays, when nobody works or goes to school. Large crowds gather for the political holidays: Labor Day (May 1), *Madaraka* Day (June 1), Moi Day (October 10), Kenyatta Day (October 20), and *Jamhuri* Day (December 12). On these occasions, the entertainment begins at about nine o'clock in the morning. Traditional dances are performed in front of the president, other important men in the government, or the village chief. Kenyan children play a big role in these celebrations. School choirs sing, and sometimes schoolchildren put on plays. The main speeches begin around ten-thirty or eleven o'clock. Afterward, there might be a soccer game. By early afternoon, everything is over.

The biggest holiday is Jamhuri Day, Kenya's national independence day. People flock to stadiums and parks to listen to speeches by political leaders. The speakers remind Kenyans how they achieved freedom after more than 60 years of British rule. Everyone is expected to listen to all the speeches, and anyone caught working is picked up by the police. In the cities, the military takes part in the celebration. Jets fly overhead

In preparation for a dance, boys heat their drums. The heat tightens the skin on the drums, producing a better sound.

while troops march in formation. Vendors sell goods and food they have prepared for the occasion.

Madaraka Day marks the anniversary of the day Kenyans actually began to run their own nation. In Nairobi, huge crowds gather to see the president and listen to what he has to say about their country. People who

can't come to Nairobi aren't left out. The president pre-
pares a speech that regional officials read in every part of
the country. He gives his people a gift: the promise of
better jobs or more schools or anything else the nation
needs. Sometimes, he will free political prisoners.

Schoolchildren are an important part of this celebration. Some read poems they have created. The poems tell how they feel about their country and how proud they are to be Kenyans. Other children, wearing their traditional clothing, perform special dances for the president and government officials.

Another big holiday is Kenyatta Day, which honors Jomo Kenyatta, the man who led Kenya in its fight for independence. Kenyatta is called the father of his country, just as George Washington is called the father of the United States. The president's speech on this national holiday is about the achievements Kenya has made and the goals still to be reached. Jomo Kenyatta is every child's hero, and Kenyan children join together to praise him. They sing, dance, and recite poetry in his honor.

Children look forward to other holidays—and not just because they don't have to go to school. Labor Day, for example, rewards all workers with a day off, and rural Kenyans who work in the cities often visit their villages. It's a happy time when families can be together.

Kenyans observe some of the holidays we celebrate in the United States. On January 1, the president gives a speech about his new policies for the coming year. The rest of the day is spent visiting friends. Good Friday and Easter Monday are two more holidays. Easter festivities last four days in Kenya. Christians go to church and get

Dancers wearing clog shoes and monkey headdresses celebrate a national holiday in western Kenya.

together for special meals with their relatives. Many children get new clothes for the occasion.

Christmas Day is another time when people go to church. Young people put on religious plays for little children. Choirs from different schools have singing competitions. Afterward, Father Christmas gives each child a new toy. Parents have already given them something new to wear.

Kenyans observe two holidays not celebrated in the United States. Boxing Day, December 26, is a British tradition, begun with the custom of giving a Christmas box to servants, the mailman, the man who delivers the newspaper, et cetera. The Muslim festival *Eid al-Fitr,* which means breaking of the fast, follows *Ramadan.* During the month of Ramadan, Muslims fast from sunrise to sundown every day. Eid al-Fitr is a holiday for everyone in Kenya. People who have Muslim friends visit their homes and share food with them.

A Happy Festival

Each ethnic group in Kenya has its own festivals and rituals to celebrate major events in their culture. They sing, dance, and feast at these ceremonies, and children have the best time of all.

The favorite ceremony of Pokot girls is the coming-of-age ceremony, when they're around 12 years old.

The morning of the initiation rites, all the women in the village gather around the initiates. The young girls kneel and bury their faces in their hands while each mother talks about her daughter's character. One mother says her daughter "is really bad. She has a big mouth." The mother asks, "When she marries someone, won't she take all those words with her?" The other women tell the girl how she should behave when she marries.

After everyone has been talked about, the girls go home and get ready for their big day. People come from miles around dressed in their best clothes to honor the initiates and to dance to joyful songs. The initiates come to the dance area decked out in their finest clothes and most colorful beads. Their bodies glisten with ocher, a red clay, and ghee, an animal fat, and their jewelry glitters in the sun. They proudly join the other women dancing the *adongo,* a line dance in which the women face off against the men. The initiates are now considered adults and ready to marry.

6. Kenyan Homes, Family Life, and Food

Kenyans value their family and friends. Most families are large. It is not unusual for children to have five or six brothers and sisters, and some have even more. They often think of their cousins as brothers and sisters as well. In rural areas, uncles and aunts are thought of as fathers and mothers. Children speak of "my father and my other father and my other father." Kenyan children grow up knowing they are loved by a lot of people.

Most Kenyans, about 80 percent, live in rural parts of the country. Some are still traditional herders, but more are farmers. Many young people go to the cities and towns to look for work. When they find jobs, they send money home to parents and relatives. They also go back every now and then to help on the family farms or to attend important tribal rituals and celebrations.

The Masai, Traditional Herders

The Masai, the famous warrior tribe, are herders whose lives center on their cattle, the changing seasons, and their children. They live in small settlements. Several

Inside a Masai kraal. The hut is made from branches, twigs, grass, and cow dung mixed with ashes.

families build a kraal, which is a circle of ten or twelve huts surrounded by a thornbush fence. The men and older boys gather branches from thornbushes to build the fence. The two-inch-long thorns that grow on the thin branches of this savannah bush are as sharp as barbed wire. The men tie the branches together and stand them up in a wide circle to protect their livestock against wild animals and cattle thieves. At night, cattle, goats, and sheep sleep in the center of the kraal.

The women build igloo-shaped huts. First they make a frame from branches, twigs, and grass. Then they mix cow dung with ashes and plaster it onto the frame. When the mixture dries and bakes in the sun, it is as strong as cement. The huts are too low to stand in, and the only light and fresh air come from the door opening. But they keep the Masai warm and dry during the rainy season.

Masai children have a lot of freedom when they are young. Boys practice running and throwing, and they pretend to be herdsmen. Three- and four-year-olds get ready to learn to herd cattle by carrying a stick in their hands. When they are a little older, they each carry a longer stick with a sharp point and pretend it is a spear. As soon as a boy turns 12, he can carry a spear with a short blade. Boys spend most of their time looking after cattle. They learn how to tell if an animal is sick just by looking at its hide. The Masai think of their cattle as friends. They know each animal's personality, its special humps and colors, and even the tone of its voice.

Girls play with dolls and learn to make their own jewelry, clothing, and household articles. When they are about nine years old, they spend less time playing and learn how to cook, clean house, and take care of babies.

Their chores include milking the cows, getting water, gathering firewood, and plastering their hut. If their father has no sons, they care for the sheep and calves, but they don't like to do this.

A Masai girl can marry when she is about 12 years old. During a special coming-of-age ceremony, the hair is shaved from her head, and she gives away all her old clothing and ornaments. Friends and relatives come to the girl's kraal for a celebration. An ox is killed for the feast, and cow's blood is mixed with sour milk to make a drink called *asaroi*. There is much singing and dancing, and the girl receives gifts such as gourds filled with milk. Sometimes she may get her own calf.

Masai boys have their coming-of-age ceremony when they are about 16 years old. They begin by showing how brave and strong they are. In the old days, they had to kill a lion with their spear, but it's now against the law to kill a lion unless a person is attacked. Today, they perform other brave deeds, such as spending the night outside the kraal under the stars with not even a spear to protect them.

Two months before a boy's ceremony is to take place, he and his family begin preparations. They must collect honey, which is made into honey beer for the elders and guests. The boy gathers ostrich plumes and eagle feathers for the headdress he will make. Two days before the ceremony, his head is shaved and all his belongings are given away. To symbolize his new life, he must start again with everything new. The day before the ceremony, he searches for a special African olive sapling (a very young tree), which is planted next to his hut.

The new warriors celebrate in grand style. They put on red togas and cover their bodies from head to toe with a mixture of ground ocher and fat or water. Then they draw designs in the wet ocher with their fingertips or a stick. They wear beaded necklaces, earrings, belts, and anklets that their mothers and girlfriends have made for them. An ox is slaughtered for the feast. The young warriors sit around a circle, and elders smear the foreheads of the young men with fatty meat. Then the elders offer them a bite of the meat. Finally, the elders spit honey beer on the youths.

Unlike Masai girls, warriors don't marry until the boys in their age-set become junior elders. That takes more than ten years. Like all other stages of Masai life, there is a special ceremony before the warriors become junior elders. At the close of the ceremony, they each go to their home kraals to begin a new life.

The Pokot Farmers

The Pokot people who live in the hills rising from the Great Rift Valley in western Kenya are farmers. Everyone goes to bed when it gets dark, since there is no elec-

An everyday chore for Kenyan children: hauling water from rivers and streams.

tricity. As soon as dawn begins to light up the sky, they get up. All Pokot children have chores. Cherop, a ten-year-old girl, begins her day by bringing water to her family's hut. She fills a gourd from water flowing in a channel cut into the hillside. Then she pours it into a pot on the fire. When the water boils, her mother sifts in ground maize, stirring the mixture with a long wooden spoon until it thickens. Cherop and her brothers and sisters either eat this cornmeal porridge, called *uji,* for breakfast or drink *chai,* tea mixed with milk and sugar.

Before Cherop goes to school, she has to milk the goats, sweep the dirt floor of their hut, and collect chicken eggs. Chickens live in the same huts as the families. When there is no school, Cherop takes care of her younger brothers and sisters. She makes sure they do their chores, such as picking ticks out of the sheep's ears. She also helps the older girls sew and repair clothes, or she makes her own jewelry.

Cherop and her brothers and sisters like to go to the fields to chase away birds that try to eat the crops. They sit on a raised platform in the middle of the field and throw stones or mud balls at the birds. Sometimes it gets a little tiring sitting there all day, but Cherop has fun being a human scarecrow.

At the end of the day, Cherop's family has *ugali* for dinner. Ugali is made from maize flour and water. The mixture thickens as it simmers over the fire. Another pot of boiling water is for cooking beans or collard greens. When it's time to eat, everyone pinches off a piece of cooled ugali, molds it into the shape of a

These Kenyan mothers enjoy wearing colorful clothes and skill-fully made ornaments.

spoon, and scoops the beans or greens from the pot. After dinner, the girls and boys sit around the fire and ask each other riddles or listen to a storyteller recount tales of their ancestors.

Farmers in Eastern Kenya

Farming families in eastern Kenya live a different kind of life from those in the west. It rains more near the coast, and farmers plant a wider variety of crops. They grow grains such as rice, millet, and maize; root crops such as sweet potatoes, yams, and taro; and a variety of fruits such as bananas, oranges, papaws (papayas), and mangoes. Coconut palms provide food, drink, oil, and material for thatching roofs and making ropes and baskets.

Salomé, an 11-year-old girl, helped build her family house. She collected roots and stems from mangrove trees in the swampy land along the coast. Mangrove poles make a good framework. When the frame was in place, the fun part began. Salomé and her family jumped into a pile of red-clay soil, water, and grass, and they mixed it together with their feet. Then they plastered this mixture onto the frame. Finally they put on a roof of palm leaves.

Families who have money to buy materials build

more modern houses. Floors are concrete instead of dirt. Walls are built with cement blocks or bricks. Roofs are made from corrugated iron.

Most of the farmers in eastern Kenya, no matter what their income, enjoy wearing brightly colored clothes. Women tie colorful bandannas around their heads to protect themselves from the hot sun and dusty roads. Those who have babies use a *kanga,* the bright piece of cloth that often has a proverb woven into it. They tie it across their back or hip and use it as a sling for carrying their baby. Some women wrap a large rectangle of colorful cloth around their body like a sarong. This is called a *kitenge.* Others wear cotton dresses or skirts and blouses.

Most men in this part of Kenya wear shorts or long pants and a dashiki, a loose shirt printed in bright African designs. A few in the remote countryside dress in the *kanzu,* the long white robe that is also worn by Muslims in the coastal cities. Almost everyone, both men and women, either goes barefoot or wears flat-soled sandals.

Kenyan Food

The kinds of food Kenyans eat vary throughout the country. Milk is the principal food of herding families in the more remote areas. They also make soups, to which they add certain roots and barks. Meat from sheep or goats is eaten on special occasions. Farming families enjoy a wider variety of food. In addition to ugali once or twice a day, they eat vegetables such as yams, beans, and potatoes. Meat is a luxury that they have once a week or so.

Fish is the main food of the El Molo people, near Lake Turkana. Every once in a while, they eat crocodile or turtle meat, as well as certain birds. Kenyans who live around Lake Victoria also eat a lot of fish, along with vegetables and grains. There are many kinds of fish in the Indian Ocean for coastal residents. They also enjoy a lot of fruits: mangoes, papaws, pineapples, bananas, oranges, and limes. Mombasa is famous for its spicy curry dishes.

Nairobi has just about any kind of food. Lamb and beef from western Kenya and fresh fruits and vegetables from the highlands north of the city provide Nairobians who can afford it a wide variety of food. Most people, however, eat ugali, maize, and beans for dinner, just as rural Kenyans do. On special occasions, they roast a goat. Anyone who wants American food can buy pizza, hamburgers, and french fries in Nairobi.

Here are two easy Kenyan recipes you can prepare for your family and friends.

Market day in a rural Kenyan village.

Plantains* in Coconut Milk

3 to 4 peeled plantains, sliced
¼ tsp. salt
1 tsp. curry powder
½ tsp. cinnamon
⅛ tsp. cloves
1 to 2 cups coconut milk

☛Combine all ingredients except coconut milk in a heavy saucepan. ☛Pour in 1 cup of coconut milk and simmer over low heat until plantains are very tender and milk is absorbed. ☛Add more coconut milk, if necessary. ☛Serve hot. ☛Serves 4–6. ☛Try this with curries or with fish.

*Plantains are a kind of banana that can be cooked.

Mango Snow

4 unripe mangoes, peeled and thinly sliced
2 tbs. sugar

☛In a pot with just enough water to cover the bottom, steam the mango slices until they are very soft. ☛Keep a close watch to make sure the water doesn't simmer away, leaving the mangoes to burn or stick. ☛Puree the cooked mangoes in a blender or food processor along with the sugar, or mash mangoes and sugar together until all lumps are gone. ☞Serve immediately or chill.

Variation: ☞Whip 1 cup of heavy cream and fold it into chilled mango puree before serving.

☞Serves 6.

7. *Education, Kenyan Style*

When Kenya was a colony of Great Britain, children of the white settlers attended modern schools with trained teachers, lots of books, and well-equipped playgrounds. Kenyan children went to makeshift schools, usually run by Christian missionaries. There were few books, not enough desks, and the playgrounds were often just patches of dirt. Many children never went to school at all because they lived too far away or their parents needed their help at home.

After independence in 1963, the Kenyan government took over the mission schools. President Kenyatta believed schools were the key to his nation's future. But the new government did not have the funds to build additional schools. He urged people to raise money and help build new schools themselves. They did, and the new schools were called harambee schools, after the national motto, "Let's pull together." Kenyans still donate money and labor to build harambee schools, mostly in rural areas.

Education is important to Kenyans. Many children walk barefoot more than one hour each day to get to school. Parents must sacrifice to pay school fees so their children can get an education. When there are five or six

Children in front of their school in the highlands. They wear hats to keep their heads warm in the cold morning air, although most go barefoot.

children in a family, parents often cannot afford to pay for each child's education. The oldest goes through school at a normal pace. Younger brothers and sisters are often held back in the free primary grades until the parents have enough money to pay additional school fees. Older children help pay to educate their younger siblings when they graduate and go to work.

The School System

Kenya's school year is divided into three three-month terms with a one-month vacation in between each term. There are eight years of primary school and four years of secondary school. Primary grades are called standards, and secondary grades are called forms.

Children enter standard one when they are six or seven years old. At the end of standard eight, they take an examination for the Kenya Certificate of Primary Education (KCPE). Everybody wants to do well on the KCPE exam so he or she can get into a good secondary school. Many schools hold review classes during vacations or on Saturdays to help the students pass. The test is so important that, before the exam, communities hold church meetings to pray for the success of their students.

There are two kinds of secondary schools: government-aided schools and harambee schools. Students with the highest KCPE scores are given a place in the government schools. Most of these are boarding schools, which means that students move away from home and live in dormitories. They begin in the first form, about the same as ninth grade in U.S. schools. Government schools are generally well supplied, and the teachers are trained and experienced. Everyone wants to go to a government-aided secondary school, but only one out of every four who applies is accepted.

Students with lower KCPE scores go to harambee schools or to a youth polytechnic (a trade school), or they drop out of school altogether. Seventy-five percent of Kenya's secondary schools are harambee schools. Some of them look like the kind of school Abraham Lincoln attended: They have dirt floors, handmade desks, and no glass in the windows. These schools must make do with much less than government-aided schools have. There are never enough desks and supplies to go around. Two or three students share one desk. They must also share the few textbooks in the classroom. Science classes have little equipment for experiments. And qualified teachers are hard to find.

But students work very hard. They hope to earn good scores on another exam all students must take, this time for the Kenya Certificate of Secondary Education (KCSE). Those with the highest scores are admitted to

A model farm, where boys and young men live for a week at a time to learn modern farming methods.

the university or a good technical college. Others look for jobs or go to youth polytechnics.

Youth polytechnics teach skills in such fields as masonry, carpentry, metal working, typing, business management, sewing, and agriculture. The programs last around two years, but many students take twice as long to graduate. Every few months, they drop out because they don't have enough money for school fees. As soon as they earn enough money, they return.

A Typical Day in Primary School

Joseph lives with his grandmother in the small village of Kapchebau, which overlooks the Great Rift Valley in western Kenya. Until he was six years old, he stayed down in the valley with his parents. But it was hot there, and mosquitoes brought malaria, a disease that makes people feverish and weak. So when he was old enough to go to school, he moved in with his grandmother. He misses his parents, but he visits them during school vacations.

Joseph gets up every morning when the sun rises to do chores. After breakfast, he puts on his uniform and walks to school, where he has more chores to do. Like all Kenyan students, Joseph must help clean up his school. While the girls sweep the classroom floor and straighten the desks, Joseph and the other boys weed the yard and slash grass that has grown too high. Students even bring their own cleaning supplies to school, such as mops, brooms, and soap.

When the bell rings, Joseph lines up for parade. The headmaster (principal) and teachers make announcements and check everyone's uniform. Joseph looks down at his belt. Last week he forgot it, and was sent home. He listens to the teachers call out the names of the boys and girls who have misbehaved. He's glad he has been good, because punishments are announced in front of the whole school. Students who have really been bad must kneel on the ground and get caned. Others have to trim the bushes, fetch water, or pull weeds.

Classes begin around eight-thirty. Joseph is in the fourth standard and studies both English and Swahili grammar. He picked up a little English during his first three years in school, but now he has to learn it well because soon all of his classes will be taught in English. He also studies the history of East Africa, world geography, mathematics, and religion. He looks forward to the 15-minute break in the morning, and he can hardly wait for lunch.

Kenyan children eat simple lunches. Some days, Joseph has a banana or a cold sweet potato. Other days he eats ugali or maize and beans. During lunch hour, Joseph and his friends play ball games or go for walks in the bush. If they're lucky, they find wild fruit to eat.

If they're really lucky, they'll see termites flying around a termite mound. Termites are a real treat, and as soon as the children catch one, they pop it into their mouths.

After lunch, there are two more hours of classes. Then "Games" begin. This is like physical education. Depending on the season, everyone plays "athletics" (track and field) and volleyball. Sometimes boys have a soccer game and girls play netball (women's basketball). At four or five o'clock everyone goes home.

A Harambee Secondary School

Memusi is in the first form at a harambee secondary school 150 miles north of Nairobi. Villagers made mud bricks and built the school themselves. The local church donated money for the corrugated iron roof and a few desks, and parents raised money to buy more desks. A thornbush fence surrounds the rectangular classroom building, a girls' dormitory, and a mud hut with a thatched roof, which is the kitchen. The boys live in the village.

Memusi and the other girls who live in the dormitory get up early. After a study period from seven o'clock to eight, all students gather in the yard for parade. The headmaster speaks, everyone sings an anthem, and the Kenyan flag is raised. Then it's time to tidy up the school.

Students at a harambee secondary school. Girls live in a dormitory at the school, while boys live in the village nearby.

Classes begin as soon as chores are finished. Memusi's first class is English. She tries hard to listen to the teacher above the crowing of the rooster. The window in the classroom is broken, and it is easy to hear what's happening outside. During geography, her least favorite class, she watches the cows wander by until the teacher calls on her. Memusi stands beside her desk, but she has no answer to give. She's happy when class is over and it's time for morning break.

Mathematics class comes after the break. Memusi copies into her exercise book the problems the teacher writes on the blackboard. Then she tries to solve them while the teacher checks other students' homework. Since there's a paper shortage in Kenyan schools, Memusi works out the answers on the palm of her hand or on scraps of paper. After mathematics, she has either home economics, first aid, or nutrition.

Then it's lunchtime. All morning, the school cook has tended an enormous pot set on three stones over a fire. She has thrown maize, beans, potatoes, and carrots into the boiling water. Day students have brought vegetables from home to add to the mixture. The cook serves a ladleful to each student, and they sit on the ground in a patch of shade to eat. With the meal, they drink water from the school rain tank. Memusi is glad it has rained lately. Otherwise she and the other girls would have to go down to the stream and bring back pots full of water.

Classes continue in the afternoon. Memusi's science class is taught by a U.S. Peace Corps worker. The school had no lab equipment until her teacher's parents sent two microscopes. At the end of science class, another teacher comes to the classroom to teach Swahili literature, her favorite class. Then she has religious studies or crafts and business.

At four o'clock, classes end and students head for

the playing field. At five, the boys go home and the girls have dinner. When it gets dark, kerosene lanterns are lit. Everyone studies from seven until ten, and then it's time for bed. All 30 girls sleep in one large room. But Memusi doesn't mind. It's much bigger than the hut she sleeps in with her family.

This is a very long day. But Kenyans are used to working hard in school. They feel fortunate to be there. Kenyan children study more subjects than most American schoolchildren do. At the end of each term, they must take an exam in each subject, and at the end of primary and secondary schools, they take the important certificate exams. So Kenyan schoolchildren know they must work hard in order to do well on all these tests.

8. Sports, Fun, and Good Times

When most people think of Kenyan sports, they picture a runner zooming in front of the pack to win still another long-distance race. Some of the best long-distance runners in the world come from Kenya. Kenyans have won 24 Olympic medals in men's running events. They have also been among the top finishers in many 26-mile marathons. Ibrahim Hussein has won the Boston Marathon twice (1988 and 1991) as well as the Honolulu and New York City marathons in 1987. His countryman Douglas Wakiihuri has won four of the eight marathons he has entered.

Kipchoge Keino, the first great Kenyan runner, is a national hero. Many Kenyan boys began competitive running after watching or reading about him. Henry Rono, Mike Boit, and John Ngugi are well-known internationally and have also inspired young runners. Kenyans run barefoot races at school and in local meets, and many dream of becoming their nation's next great runner.

Joseph Kibor is a young runner with a great future. He has been racing barefoot most of his life. In primary school, he and his friends made their own running track. They cut lanes out of the thick grass with *pangas,* machetelike knives. His secondary school was not on ground flat enough for a track. So he raced two miles every morning up a steep hill from the village where he lives. After school, he ran three miles crosscountry, and on the weekends he added more miles.

Shortly before his 17th birthday, he entered his first important track meet. He had to sell a goat for the seven dollars to pay for the bus trip from his home to the meet. This left him no money to buy running shoes. Joseph ran the 10,000-meter race (25 laps) barefoot and finished third. That earned him a spot on Kenya's team for the 1990 Commonwealth Games in Aukland, New Zealand. He was the youngest male to represent Kenya in a major competition and finished fifth. After the race, Joseph said, "My feet are painful now. I do think shoes would have helped."

Football

Football, known as soccer in the U.S., is the national team sport. It is played by boys and men on any plot of level ground, from grassy parks in Nairobi to corn-stubble fields in rural areas. There are soccer teams in most schools and towns, and thousands of Kenyans pack stadiums for weekend matches between teams from

Kenya's towns and cities. The Kenyan national team, called the Harambee Stars, competes against teams from other African countries and Europe. They also play in the Commonwealth Games, which bring together athletes from Britain's former colonies, such as Canada, Australia, New Zealand, and India.

Toys and Games

Most Kenyans don't have much money, so they make their own toys. Anything can be a toy. Girls play jacks using stones or berries. They make dolls out of scraps of cloth and yarn, from banana tree fibers, or even mud. Boys and girls make balls from anything that's handy. For example, they twine together fibers from banana trees, or they pack old newspapers in plastic bags.

Amazing toys are made out of wire and old clothes hangers, such as tiny bicycles with wheels that turn and toy cars with wheels and a steering column. Every Easter, boys race the cars they've made through their neighborhood streets in Nairobi. They hold their own "safari rally" at the same time some of the world's best rally drivers are racing all over Kenya in the world championship Safari Rally. Besides cars, boys build their own skateboards out of scraps of wood. If they're near a river, children scoop up clay and model animals,

A toy car takes shape under the skillful hands of a young Kenyan.

cars, and dolls. They also collect slender tree branches
and bend them into circles. Girls use them as Hula
Hoops, while boys stand the hoops on end and roll them
with sticks.

Kenyan children play some of the same games
American children do: pat-a-cake; one potato, two

potato; hide-and-seek; grown-ups. Girls like to braid each other's hair, or they make pretend hair out of long grass. They braid it, oil it, and create fancy hairdos. They also like to jump rope and sing together. When they get older, they make up love songs to sing to their boyfriends.

Boys have fun hunting birds or sliding down slopes on banana leaves. A favorite game of Masai boys is warriors and lions. They pretend a lion has attacked their herd and they are warriors chasing it. Sometimes they have mock battles and throw cattle dung at one another.

Movies and TV

Young people who live in Nairobi have something in common with American youngsters: They go to the movies and watch TV. The city's 15 movie theaters show almost every popular film the United States or Great Britain has ever made. Kung fu movies are very popular, and Asian films are shown for the local Indian population. Kenyans who live in rural areas without electricity occasionally see movies, too. The government sends trucks with electric generators and movie projectors to some of the villages.

Television is available to many people in the cities.

Kenyans in Nairobi watch American television programs such as "Little House on the Prairie" and "Good Times." They can also watch news broadcasts. Until 1990, the government ran the only TV news station, Kenya Broadcasting Corporation (KBC). In this way, the government controlled all the news the people could get.

Then Nairobi gained a new television station, Kenya Television Network (KTN). KTN has brought some freedom to television news in the country. Besides offering CNN News, an American news program, it runs stories that the government would prefer people not to know about. When the government bulldozed the paper-and-tin shanties that were home to thousands of poor Kenyans in a Nairobi slum, KTN covered the story; KBC never mentioned it. Recently, when three United States senators visited Kenya, KBC only mentioned their meeting with the country's finance minister. KTN reported on the senators' criticism of Kenya's human rights record.

Modern Music and Dance

Many young people are eager to learn modern dances, such as those that teenagers do in the United States and Europe. They listen to the latest music from these countries, too. Cassette players are very popular, and even herdsmen can sometimes be seen listening to portable tape players as they herd their animals.

Some musicians are trying to create Kenya's own pop music. It is the *benga* sound, which is energetic African music sung in Swahili or other Kenyan languages. The beat imitates traditional rhythms, and the words explain traditional customs or the difficulties of urban life. President Moi discourages this kind of music. He feels that using ethnic languages is not good for the unity of the country, and he is afraid that singing about the problems of urban life might turn into criticism of his government.

9. A New Home and the Spirit of Harambee

Kenyans come to the United States for a variety of reasons. A few have settled in America permanently, but most want to return to their homeland someday. Many visitors are students seeking a college education. The universities in Kenya don't have room for everyone who wishes to attend. Those who have the money go to Great Britain or the United States for their higher education. Sometimes relatives and friends of a bright student do a harambee: They pool their money so the student can study overseas. Then when the student is educated, they hope he or she will return to Kenya and help them and their country.

Kenyan athletes have an easier time coming to U.S. colleges and universities. Many are offered scholarships to run on track-and-field teams. U.S. coaches like to have Kenyan runners on their teams because they help win championships. But not everyone believes this is fair. Some coaches think college track-and-field programs should develop U.S. runners for the Olympics. They argue that foreign runners represent their own countries in the Olympics, so U.S. coaches should spend their time and resources working with U.S. athletes only.

For a different reason Kenya's national sports federation thinks its top athletes should not be running for U.S. colleges. The loss of its best long-distance runners to the United States weakens Kenya's training system and its most famous sport.

Asylum in the United States

A few Kenyans have come to the United States because they have problems with the government and would be arrested if they stayed in their country. Gibson Kamau Kuria is an example of someone who cannot live in Kenya until the political situation changes. As a lawyer, he has represented Kenyans who have been arrested for demanding democracy and human rights. In 1987, he sued the government for imprisoning and torturing three of his clients. The government then arrested Kuria, took away his passport, and held him in prison without formal charges for ten months. There was such an international outcry over this that President Moi was forced to release him.

Kuria had become a hero in the international human rights movement. In 1988, he won the Robert F. Kennedy Human Rights Award. Because the Kenyan government still held his passport at that time, Kuria was unable to travel to New York for the award ceremony. So Robert F. Kennedy's daughter Kerry went to Kenya to present him with the award.

Kuria continued defending people who spoke out for human rights. In 1990, he learned he was about to be arrested again. Friends told him that the police were waiting for him at his office, his home, and the courthouse. He went into hiding at the U.S. embassy in Nairobi. After intense diplomatic talks, Kenyan officials allowed him to fly to the United States. Kuria is now a visiting scholar at Harvard Law School, and he continues to pursue his quest for multiparty democracy in Kenya.

A National Chess Champion

Dr. Ed Karanja and his wife, Waithira, live in the United States under happier circumstances. Dr. Karanja came to this country as an exchange student from Kenya, received a college scholarship, and earned his Ph.D. degree. He teaches philosophy at Brooklyn College in New York City, and his wife teaches English at City College.

Their son, Kangugi—or K.K., as he prefers to be called—was born in New York in 1974. On his seventh

Chess champion K.K. with fans during a 1986 tour in Kenya.

birthday, his father took him to a toy store in their Harlem neighborhood and asked him to pick out three games. K.K. chose Scrabble, backgammon, and chess. His father tried to talk him out of the chess set because he thought he was too young. But K.K. insisted on buying it, and he taught himself to play the game. Then he taught his father, mother, and older sister. When K.K.

was eight years old, he entered the National Primary Championship and won.

K.K. has been winning ever since. He has earned many titles and is considered one of the top chess players in the United States. He has also introduced chess to children of minority groups, very few of whom have had an opportunity to play the game.

Freedom and Respect

How do Kenyan immigrants like life in the United States? Their reactions are mixed. All agree that the pace of life is very different from that in Kenya. Americans eat fast, they talk fast, they drive fast. There are many more things to do here, and some Kenyans feel that they can barely keep up. Students prefer the U.S. system of education. What they learn is more practical and down to earth, and they don't have to study so many different subjects.

Everyone likes the freedom of being able to say whatever he or she feels like saying. Kenya is the kind of place where people are careful of what they say and to whom they say it. They are afraid to confide even in their closest friends, for fear someone will listen and repeat the conversation, and they might end up in jail.

Kenyan immigrants feel quite different and very apart from the rest of the people, including African

Americans. Sometimes they run into racial prejudice, but as soon as people learn they are from Kenya, they are generally treated very well. Some African Americans envy the Kenyans living here because they are so respected. One young Kenyan tries to ignore racial prejudice and be friendly with everyone. She believes prejudice is ignorance and that when people get to know one another, they no longer have reason to be prejudiced.

Kenyans who come to this country bring the spirit of harambee, which has been such an important part of their lives. The United States might do well to adopt a similar policy of working together to build a more harmonious society. In the same way, if the people of Kenya can continue to "pull together" in peace, their nation can set an example for other African countries in their quest for a better way of life.

Appendix A

Kenyan Embassy and Other Offices in the United States and Canada

Consulates, embassies, and tourist offices offer assistance to Americans and Canadians who wish to learn more about Kenya. For information and resource materials, contact any of the following.

U.S. Embassy, Consulate, and Tourist Offices

Kenya Embassy
2249 R Street NW
Washington, DC 20008
(202) 387-6101

Kenya Consulate and Tourist Office
9100 Wilshire Blvd.
Suite 111-112
Beverly Hills, CA 90212
(310) 274-6635

Kenya Tourist Office
424 Madison Avenue
New York, NY 10017
(212) 486-1300

Canadian High Commission

Kenya High Commission
415 Laurier Avenue East
Ottawa, Ontario K1N 6R4
(613) 563-1773

Appendix B

Say It in Swahili

The Swahili language evolved along the East African coast from the intermixing of African Bantu with Arabic. The word "Swahili" comes from the Arabic word for "coast." Swahili is an easy language to pronounce if you remember a few rules. Syllables always end with a vowel, and the stress is always on the next-to-last syllable. Vowels are pronounced as follows: a=ah as in father; e=ay as in say; i=ee as in see; o=oh as in hoe; u=oo as in too.

English	*Swahili*	*Pronunciation*
hello	jambo	JAH-mbo
good-bye	kwaheri	kwah-HAY-ree
yes	naam	nah-AHM
no	la	LAH
please	tafadhali	tah-fah-DHAH-lee
thank you	asante	ah-SAH-ntay
today	leo	LAY-oh
tomorrow	kesho	KAY-shoh
yesterday	jana	JAH-nah
good	mwema	MWAY-mah
bad	mbaya	MBAH-yah
big	kubwa	KOO-bwah
small	kidogo	kee-DOH-goh
man	mwamamume	mwah-mah-MOO-may
woman	mwanamke	mwah-NAH-mkay
child	mtoto	MTOH-toh
boy	mbulana	mboo-LAH-nah
girl	msichana	msee-CHAH-nah
father	baba	BAH-bah
mother	mama	MAH-mah
quickly	upesi	oo-PAY-see
slowly	pole pole	POH-lay POH-lay
lion	simba	SEE-mbah

giraffe	twiga	TWEE-gah
hippopotamus	kiboko	kee-BOH-koh
elephant	tembo	TEE-mboh
monkey	nyani	NYAH-nee
zebra	punda milia	POO-ndah mee-LEE-ah

one	moja	MOH-jah
two	mbili	MBEE-lee
three	tatu	TAH-too
four	nne	NNAY
five	tano	TAH-noh
six	sita	SEE-tah
seven	saba	SAH-bah
eight	nane	NAH-nay
nine	tisa	TEE-sah
ten	kumi	KOO-mee
eleven	kumi na moja	KOO-mee nah MOH-jah
twelve	kumi na mbili	KOO-mee nah MBEE-lee

Glossary

age-set — all the boys, or girls, born during a period of three or four years

anthropologist (an-throh-POL-oh-jist) — a person who studies the origins and development of human beings

athletics — track and field

bride price — the customary payment a man makes to his future wife's family

chador (SHAH-dor) — a black garment that covers a Muslim woman from head to toe

chai (CHY) — tea mixed with milk and sugar

dashiki (dah-SHEE-kee) — a loose shirt printed in bright African designs

duka (DOO-kah) — a small shop

escarpment (es-KARP-ment) — a steep cliff

ethnic group — a group of people who have their own language, culture, history, and religion

excavate — uncover by digging

ghee (GEE) — animal fat

harambee (hah-RAHM-bee) — a Swahili word meaning "Let's pull together"

initiation rites — ceremonies in which boys and girls take on the responsibilities of adults

kanga (KAHN-ga) — a long piece of cloth wrapped around a woman's back or hip

kanzu (KAHN-zoo) — a full-length white robe worn by a Muslim man in Kenya

kitenge (kee-TEN-gah) — a large rectangle of colorful cloth that is tied around a woman's body like a sarong

maize (MAYZ) — a white, large-kernel corn

malaria — the disease carried by certain mosquitoes that makes a person feverish and weak

mangrove trees — tropical trees having branches that send down many roots, which look like additional trunks. Mangroves grow along tidal shores on Kenya's coast.

millet (MILL-et) — the very small grain of a kind of cereal grass

missionary — a person who goes to a foreign country to do religious and humanitarian work

monsoon (mahn-SOON) — a seasonal wind in the Indian Ocean and southern Asia

Muslim (MUHZ-lim) — a person who follows the religion of Islam, who believes in one god, Allah, and in the prophet Muhammad

nomads — people who move from place to place to provide food or pasture for their animals

ocher (OHK-er) — red earth containing clay and iron oxide

oral history — the history of a people passed down from one generation to the next by spoken words

panga (PAHN-ga) — a machetelike knife with a sharp blade

poachers — people who hunt animals illegally

proto — earliest form of something

pyrethrum (pie-REE-thrum) — an insecticide made from dried chrysanthemum heads

safari (sah-FAH-ree) — journey or hunting expedition

savannah (sah-VAN-ah) — a broad area of grasslands with scattered trees

shamba (SHAM-bah) — small family farm

sisal (SY-zal) — a fiber used to make rope

Swahili (swah-HEE-lee) — the language that evolved along the East Africa coast from the intermixing of African Bantu and Arabic; the word also refers to the coastal people who speak Swahili

tradition — the handing down of beliefs, customs, and stories from parents to children, especially by word of mouth or by practice

tribal — characteristic of a particular group of people who have their own language, culture, history, and religion

trona (TROH-nah) — soda ash, a mineral used in making glass and detergents

tropical — of regions near the equator

ugali (oo-GAH-lee) — a common Kenyan food made from maize flour and water cooked in a big pot over a hot fire until it is thicker than mashed potatoes

uji (OO-jee) — porridge made from maize flour and water. It resembles Cream of Wheat

Selected Bibliography

Abrahams, Roger D. *African Folktales: Traditional Stories of the Black World.* New York: Pantheon Books, 1983.

Adamson, Joy. *Born Free: A Lioness of Two Worlds.* New York: Vintage Books, 1974.

Dinesen, Isak. *Out of Africa.* New York: Vintage Books, 1972.

Kaplan, Irving, with Margarita K. Dobert. *Area Handbook for Kenya.* Washington, D.C.: U.S. Government Printing Office, 1985.

Kenyatta, Jomo. *Facing Mount Kenya.* New York: Vintage Books, 1965.

Lamb, David. *The Africans.* New York: Random House, 1982.

Maren, Michael. *The Land and People of Kenya.* New York: J. P. Lippincott, 1989.

Meyerhoff, Elizabeth L. "The Threatened Ways of Kenya's Pokot People." *National Geographic* 161, no. 1 (January 1982).

Ochieng', William R. *A History of Kenya.* London: Macmillan Publishers, Ltd., 1985.

Saitoti, Tepilit Ole. *Maasai.* New York: Harry N. Abrams, Inc., 1990.

Turnbull, Colin. *Tradition and Change in African Tribal Life.* Cleveland: World Publishing Co., 1966.

Ungar, Sanford. *Africa: The People and Politics of an Emerging Continent.* New York: Simon & Schuster, Inc., 1986.

Index

About the Author

Joann Burch has always loved to travel and has visited every continent except Antarctica. She has a B.A. degree in English and Spanish and a Master's degree in Liberal Arts. Ms. Burch lives with her husband and three children in California and works as a freelance writer/photographer. She has published several biographies and numerous travel articles. This is her first book for Dillon Press.